THE TWO-MINUTE MESSAGE

WILLIAM FREEMAN

Straightforward Publishing
www.straightforwardco.co.uk

Straightforward Publishing
Brighton BN2 4EG

© William Freeman 2006

All rights reserved. No part of this publication may be reproduced in a retrieval system or transmitted by any means, electronic or mechanical, photocopying or other wise, without the prior permission of the copyright holder.

British Cataloguing in Publication data. A catalogue record is available for this book from the British Library.

ISBN 1903909 88 0

Printed in the United Kingdom by Webspeed Books Beds
www.webspeedbooks.com

Cover Design by Straightforward Graphics

Whilst every effort has been made to ensure that the information in this book is accurate at the time of going to print, the author and publisher recognise that the information can become out of date. The book is therefore sold on the understanding that no responsibility for errors and omissions is assumed and no responsibility is held for the information held within.

For Lucy and Tom

It would take longer than two minutes to say how special they are

If you recognise this situation, then this is the book for you

Cartoons by WALDORF
www.waldorfcartoons.com

THE TWO-MINUTE MESSAGE™
by
William Freeman

PREFACE TO REVISED EDITION

There are many challenges associated with putting across a convincing sales story and there are lots of good books telling you how to do it.

This book focuses on one important aspect of the selling process. It describes a practical technique to get your customer interested in what you have to say - the first essential step in any sales process. It then shows how you can use this technique to make your point effectively.

There's no rocket science in this book. Nor are there academic theories that look fine on paper but are difficult to apply in the real world. The Two Minute Message™ principle is based on years of practice and observation, plus a fair amount of experience and scar tissue. It makes sense and it works.

Rather than write out the long-winded 'Two Minute Message™' phrase every time, I'll abbreviate it to TMM wherever I can. I won't write TMM™ because it confuses the eye - and probably the ear if you say it out loud.

My TMM idea has been applied to all sorts of circumstances since I first wrote this book.

- a brochure message
- a press release
- a letter
- an email
- a summary of a proposal
- a business case
- a project proposal

The Two-Minute Message

- a presentation synopsis
- an interpretation of a business 'mission'
- a 'strapline' on a business card and headed notepaper
- an advertisement or PR promotion
- an internal 'culture' message
- a telephone call to get a meeting
- a 'rah-rah' sales meeting vignette
- a sales call introduction
- a sales call 'close'
- a presentation summary
- an answer to a question
- an 'elevator pitch'
- a presentation planner
- a personal CV
- a networking message

A TMM can be written or spoken. It can be proactive or reactive. There's nothing magical about the words 'two minutes' either. Your compelling message should be the minimum length it necessary to achieve its objective.

Lots of people have contributed to this book, directly and indirectly. I would like to thank my business colleagues and all my past and present clients, many of whom have suffered at the receiving end of my verbal excesses, insensitive intrusions and general ranting. My experiences with these people verified the need for the TMM technique.

I would like to thank all the students I have worked with applying the TMM process to the real world. As always, I learned far more from these people than they did from me.

My thanks too go to 'Waldorf' for providing the cartoon illustrations – try him out for your graphic needs. You can see more of his cartoon work at www.waldorfcartoons.com

The Two-Minute Message

All of the anecdotes and stories that I use in this book are based on genuine experiences so I cannot make the standard disclaimer that every character is fictitious and bears no resemblance to any person living or dead. Faces and memories were flashing through my mind as I was writing this book.

All of my 'fictitious-but-based-on-reality' characters come out of it pretty well though - apart from me that is. I wish that I had discovered the two minute message technique many years ago.

I hope you enjoy the book and that you benefit from it. Any comments that you have would be most welcome, so please feel free to contact me. Tell me your success stories and I'll include them in the next reprint. If you want help, advice or you want to use some of my TMM based services, please get in touch.

Good luck.

William Freeman
Hampton, UK
williamfreeman@btconnect.com
www.cambridge-associates.co.uk
www.TwoMinuteMessage.com

CONTENTS

1.	**HOW TO USE THIS BOOK**	15
2.	**TODAY'S BUSINESS ENVIRONMENT**	17
	- The frantic pace of business	17
	- Why a 'good sales story' isn't good enough	18
	- 'The supplier selection' challenge	20
	- 'The nervous MD'	23
	- Social calls and business calls	24
3.	**THE TWO MINUTE MESSAGE™ CONCEPT**	27
	- Definition of a TMM	27
4.	**THE TALE OF TOMMY**	29
	- The 'introductory summary'	30
	- The 'elevator' challenge	35
	- The 'set-piece' story	41
	- The 'presentation builder'	46
	- The 'networking nightmare'	50
	- The lessons for Tommy	54
5.	**APPLYING YOUR TMM**	57
	- Using a TMM to arouse interest	57
	- The TMM as a 'set-piece' message	58
	- The TMM as a 'promotional letter'	62
	- Using a TMM to plan a major presentation	64
6.	**BUILDING YOUR TMM**	65
	- The 'OATS' principle	65
	- Defining your 'SMART' objective	66
	- TMM objectives versus campaign objectives	67
	- Identifying your target audience	68
	- The 'Themes' of your message	69
	- 'Strengths' and 'Uniques'	70

7.	**THE TMM FOUR PART STRUCTURE**	73
	- Your Audience Context Statement (ACS)	73
	- Your Key Theme	76
	- Why only a single theme?	78
	- Your 'Supporting Themes'	79
	- Your 'Closing Statement'	80
8.	**YOUR RANGE OF TMM TOPICS**	83
	- The 'Three Flavours of Value'	84
	- TMM topic examples	85
9.	**FIVE KEY MESSAGES YOU WILL NEED**	87
	- Building your C7 internal TMM	89
10.	**BRAND, IMAGE & CULTURE**	91
	- Definitions	91
	- Creating your 'Strapline'	92
11.	**VIRAL MARKETING**	95
	- Your Viral Marketing mechanisms	96
	- Getting the words right	97
	- SAGE example	99
12.	**FROM TMM TO PRESENTATION**	101
	- Template for 'persuasive presentation'	102
	- Format example	103
	- The Presentation 'Close'	104
	- The 'oats for vitality model'	105
	- Learn from the theatre	106
	- The over-rehearsal myth	108
12.	**TAKING THINGS FORWARD**	109
13.	**APPENDICES**	113

The Two-Minute Message

1
HOW TO USE THIS BOOK

You see, I was right about the 'no rocket science' but don't worry, this section isn't as daft or patronising as it might seem.

You could read this book in a single sitting - in fact, I recommend that approach. If you are reading it your local bookshop, you could brazen things out until you have finished - but I suggest you buy the book because I want you to read it a second, and even a third time.

Some people have told me that they enjoyed reading it whilst soaking in the bath at the end of a long day, with a favourite cocktail to hand.

The second time you read the book, have a pen in your hand and scribble notes on it. Use your highlighter pens and put swathes of colour all over the place. Ignore what you were told at school about not writing on books. This is a workbook; it isn't a trophy to display on your bookshelf or on coffee table.

Besides, it isn't an expensive book. Once you've written all over this copy and torn out some pages to keep close to your heart, you can always buy another one. If you live in the UK you can get a special deal via my website at www.cambridge-associates.co.uk

The overall message that I am trying to impress you with is a very simple one.

I haven't defined a two minute message yet, but here's one about this book; it's a two minute message about the relevance and value of the two minute message process.

The Two-Minute Message

Here it is. Phew – glad I left out the trademark signs in that last sentence!

Whatever your line of business, I'll bet your customers and prospective customers are busy people. They can't afford the time to listen to every sales story or supposed 'value proposition'. They need to believe that the time they are being asked for will prove worthwhile before they are prepared to give it.

The TMM process is a proven way of arousing your customers' interest in what you have to say. Whatever you are 'selling', that's the start you depend on. The TMM process is the best possible route to engaging with your customer and giving you the platform to sell your value.

This book explains the TMM process and shows you how and where you can use it. It contains many examples from real life that you can adapt for your own use. You will also learn how you can get direct help as and when you need it.

I encourage you to read on.

My TMM process will help you with your customer contact work, but it isn't the latest version of some magical snake oil. It won't make life 'easy' and it won't change the fact that effective communicating can be challenging and difficult.

It won't turn a complex challenge into a trivial one. Practise will turn it into a manageable one.

And one that you will relish and profit from.

2

TODAY'S BUSINESS ENVIRONMENT

The frantic pace of business

There's an incredibly frantic nature to business these days. Or so it seems to me. People are dashing about all over the place responding to the beck and call of their mobile phones, electronic pagers, palmtop computers, bleeping tie-pins and all the other wonderful gee whiz technologies that we have today.

Come to think of it, these business people aren't just dashing about while they are furiously communicating. They do it in restaurants, on trains, whilst walking the dog and when they are lying on the beach. Some people even do it while they are sitting on the lavatory.

Or so I'm told.

If we want to survive in today's business world and stay sane, we have to protect our time carefully to keep out unlimited, uncontrolled and unwanted intrusions - and it's exactly the same situation for our clients. Most business people have full diaries and demands for even more appointments and meetings.

As sales people, we should expect to work hard to get time with our clients and we must be able to justify the time that we take.

Salesmen of bygone days tell tales of how they could drift into a customer's office whenever they wanted to, and after a long and leisurely chat (and possibly some lunch) leave with a signed contract.

'Successful selling is all to do with having a good relationship', these veteran salesmen would say, 'if that's in good shape, you will have no trouble getting a slot in the customer's diary.'

There is a lot of truth in that statement, but it is only part of the story.

Why a 'good sales story' isn't good enough

As salespeople, it is crucial that we *can* tell a good story, but it counts for nothing if we can't get it in front of an appropriate audience.

The real winners in today's competitive business world are those people who can capture the imagination of their intended audience very quickly and persuade the customer to continue the discussion.

"To be successful, it's no longer good enough just to competent. You have to stir the brain cells – and the hearts – of your intended audience" Harvard Business Press 2002

Brevity is important here too. The more we add to our sales story, the more we are in danger of diluting its impact. The detail might *justify* the story but it won't attract people to it in the first place. Or make it memorable. It can have the opposite effect.

'Less is more' is phrase that my art teacher used a lot.

He wanted his students to use the minimum amount of paint and the fewest number of brush strokes to create the desired impression.

Most of us added too much colour and detail, thinking that every extra splash of colour would improve the final painting. It never did. In some cases, the blank canvas gave a better impression than the 'final' painting.

The Two-Minute Message

Adding too much detail can get you into a situation where the outcome is worse than if you had said nothing at all. I know - I've been there. Done it. Got the 'T' shirt and so on. So brevity is the key.

The Lord's Prayer has had a great impact on many parts of the world, yet it is only sixty-six words long.

The European Commission report into market forces affecting the price of cabbages is over sixty-six thousand words. There could be lots of valid detail in this document (oh yeah?) but it's unlikely to be one thousand times more memorable than the Lord's Prayer.

So if we want our message to have an impact, it must be brief and to the point.

This book will show you how to build an appealing synopsis for your critical business messages, giving you the wherewithal to engage the hearts and minds of those people you want to impress.

Once you've made a good impact and earned the extra time to tell your story in more detail, you must tell it in a compelling and persuasive manner, and give value for every minute that you take.
The TMM process will help with that too.

Here are two case examples that started me thinking about this whole process.

Case 1 - the 'supplier selection' challenge

Some time ago I did a consultancy assignment for the sales manager of a large organisation. He wanted an information system to manage his sales force and, as you would expect, many prospective suppliers were beating at his door trying to sell him their products and services.

My job was to whittle down these potential suppliers to a shortlist of two or three worthy candidates. This was good standard consultancy work from my point of view, but I suspect that my role was an irritant as far as the competing sales people were concerned. They wanted to deal with my client directly and not via an intermediary body.

They would claim that working via me could dilute their story and that I wouldn't be able to show the true value that they could offer.

Frankly, I don't blame them for having that view.

So what was the value of my role?

Graham, the client sales manager, described his situation quite simply.

"When I tell these sales people that I am too busy to see them," he said, "they seem to think that I doubt their capability - so they intensify their efforts to see me."

That made good sense to me. Any supplier worth his salt isn't going to give up without a good fight.

"They then bombard me with literature, brochures, business cases and things they call 'value propositions'," Graham continued.

The Two-Minute Message

Not forgetting reference client visits and product demonstrations, I thought. As a trained salesman, I could see the logic of what these people were doing; they wanted to prove their capabilities.

"You're absolutely right," Graham said when I pointed this out to him, "but that isn't the issue. The fact is, I *do* believe what they are saying, and I assume they *can* do everything that they claim."

I think I started to rub my eyes at this point.

"My problem," Graham went on, "is that I don't have time to let every credible supplier organisation tell its story - I must be selective. We have to spend time with every supplier we involve. We have to check references and we need to verify that their proposed solution can do what they claim. And so on. I don't know what the cost of all that time and lost business opportunity amounts to, but we're probably talking around a hundred thousand pounds per supplier."

I didn't feel this was the right moment to discuss my consultancy fee, but I could see the point Graham was making.

Senior business people want solutions that will help them, but they can't spare the time to listen to sales stories from every provider.

A friend of mine once compared this selection dilemma to buying a suit of clothes. "When you've found something you like," he said, "you'll probably buy it. If the suit fits you and if it's the right colour and the right price and so on, you are happy. It doesn't have to be the only possible suit in the world that would meet your requirements. There could be ninety-nine other racks in ninety-nine other shops with equally good offers but you don't look at all of them before you make your choice, do you?"

The Two-Minute Message

I thought that was a very good point.

I also made a note to discuss this story with my wife.

Of course, most business organisations have purchasing departments responsible for evaluating potential suppliers and their offerings, and I am not belittling the importance of that task.

However, as ambitious sales people, we want to establish personal relationships with our customer's senior executives. We want them to regard us as credible business advisors.

We must engage their interest about the value we can add to their business operations - and we must do this before our competitor takes this initiative.

After all, we don't want to be in a position like one of those ninety-nine other suits gathering dust on ninety-nine unvisited racks.

Case 2 - the nervous MD

Some years ago I acted as a mentor to the MD of a software company. I was his 'personal confidante'; someone he could share ideas with who wasn't enmeshed in any of the company politics and general infighting. A sort of business 'agony aunt', I suppose.

One of my client's sales people had arranged for my MD friend to meet the CEO of a manufacturing organisation seeking some process design software.

"Every time I am asked to do this kind of sales call," my MD client said, "I get extremely nervous". That comment rather surprised me as he struck me as a pretty confident sort of chap.

"My sales people rely on me to make a good impression that has a positive knock-on effect on our sales revenues," he continued. "If I don't succeed and if one of our competitors gets in the door, we could be locked out of this customer for several years. That's the nature of our business."

In these circumstances, making a good impact becomes pretty critical.

Being ignored (like an 'unvisited suit') doesn't necessarily happen because we have an inferior product or service. More often than not, it means that we haven't been able to tell our story to the right person, at the right time and in the right way.

For much of my sales career, business people stressed the importance of building relationships at all levels within the customer organisation. Phrases like 'relationship management', 'relationship value' and 'executive contact programmes' were all the rage.

They still are.

But client meetings must go beyond the boundaries of normal social contact.

Social calls and business calls

At one time in my career, I was an IBM sales manager looking after a major UK retail organisation. I had a team of people and we were proud of our close relationship with the customer's staff; we socialised with them, we drank with them and we had all sorts of friendly sporting contests between our two organisations.

I was surprised, therefore, when a customer executive took me to one side and advised me 'to be careful'.

"You are in danger of blurring relationship boundaries," she told me.

I must have looked puzzled so she went on to explain the differences between social and business relationships.

"Social contact tends to be casual," she said, "there is no formal agenda and the conversation is relaxed, friendly and free flowing. On the other hand, business contacts need be more structured and there has to be a purpose that *both* parties deem to be worth spending time on."

I could see what she was getting at. Too often we just popped in to 'say hello' without any other evident planned purpose. It was pleasant social stuff, but it took up time and contributed little business value as far as the customer was concerned.

The Two-Minute Message

And that is what business calls are all about. Not formality, pomposity or unnecessary structure, but making sure that *every* meeting gives the customer some value.

I remember a role play call I once did on an IBM sales training course. I had set my objective to gain lots of useful information that I could subsequently turn into sales opportunities.

"What a great sales call," I told everyone during the debriefing session. I usually made comments like that to try to boost the tutor's rating of my performance.

I then went on to tell everybody how, by my incredibly clever questioning, I had discovered one hell of a lot about the customer's organisation.

When my tutor asked me to describe the value that the *customer* had got from the meeting, I was a bit stumped. I hadn't considered that.

Establishing your credibility, purpose and potential value is vital when you are calling on someone for the first time. Actually, it is pretty important every time, and it is what differentiates a business call from a social call.

Of course, this doesn't mean that you shouldn't indulge in social banter with your client. In fact, it is vital that you do, since mentioning their holiday, kids or whatever shows that you can relate to them as individuals.

But these strands of conversation should be warm-ups (warms up?) or postscripts to a meeting or phone call, not the sole purpose of either of these events.

This is the point that my retail customer executive was making to me all those years ago.

Some people say that when you meet senior customer executives, all you have to do is ask a few key questions and they will immediately share all their problems with you. That could work in theory I suppose, but only after you have established a very close relationship with the customer and proven that you can add value.

People don't unburden themselves to anyone that happens to ask a pertinent question. They might do so with a doctor or a priest, because they recognise each of those roles as having skills that can help them. If you are in pain and you see a person wearing a white coat and carrying a stethoscope, you will tell that person your problem. You will answer any question fully and with great enthusiasm (assuming your condition allows it). You won't hold back any information.

A sales role isn't perceived as having the same kind of status (not automatically). Nevertheless, senior business people tend to be open-minded and they are happy to share confidences with consultants and other confidants whom they trust.

Establishing your credibility and your value are the foundations for establishing trust. And those things can all start from a two minute message.

The TMM process is the fastest and most effective way to get you through the 'attention', 'interest', 'engagement' cycle.

3

THE TWO MINUTE MESSAGE™ CONCEPT

Definition of a TMM

A Two Minute Message™ *is a CLEAR and CONCISE statement of value, put in a CONTEXT that is important to your target audience, which shows your CAPABILITY and CREDIBILITY and which COMPELS your target audience to COMMIT to your recommended course of action.*

Rolls of the tongue doesn't it? Go on; see how quickly you can say it.

Your TMM should meet each of the 7 'C's ('seven seas') criteria.

A TMM synopsis is the ideal starting point for any sales story or intended persuasive argument. It crystallises your story so that people understand it ('clear'). You can put it over quickly ('concise'). The challenge is to identify the content and structure your message to achieve the remaining 'C' criteria and thereby achieve your objective.

Assuming of course that you have one.

"I don't need a specific objective when I talk to customers," a salesman once told me, "I bring as wide a range of topics as I can into the conversation, and I spot those that seem to strike a chord."

To be fair to this salesman, he was pretty good at doing this. Perhaps he could spot a gleam in the eye, a blush of the cheek, a twitch in the leg, the flare of a nostril or some other neuro-linguistical sign that would go unnoticed by most of us lesser mortals.

The Two-Minute Message

But it all seemed a bit hit-and-miss to me and, come to think of it, this approach only worked with people he knew really well, never with strangers.

So there has to be a more reliable technique to 'striking that chord' with the customer and gaining the attention that you seek.

That's where the TMM technique comes in.

The next section puts the TMM process into a 'real' context.

Having done that, the remaining sections explain the process in some detail and give you tools and examples to apply to your business situation.

4

THE TALE OF TOMMY

This section of the book tells the story of Tommy, an enthusiastic, ambitious and energetic young sales representative who is keen to succeed. Just like many of the readers of this book, I'm sure.

It tells the story of how Tommy struggles through his business week trying to make best use of his time, without the benefit of a TMM.

Although this is written as a parody, a kind of fable, you will notice how the TMM technique could have helped Tommy in a variety of situations.

I would bet that you recognise quite a few of them.

Tommy gets ready

This was a critical week for Tommy. He had some important meetings set up with his prospective clients and he was determined to use this time to close some major sales.

He had spent all weekend putting his sales story together and his computer laptop presentation looked pretty good, even though he said so himself. Actually his family though so too although there were quite a few bits that they couldn't understand.

"It's very pretty daddy," Tommy's young daughter Lucy was most enthusiastic about it.

"Especially that bit where all those coloured arrows come zooming in and the music starts to play," she said.

Tommy liked that bit too.

He knew that just having a slick presentation wasn't enough. Or even a 'pretty' one. On his sales training courses he had learned how important it was to build his sales story around the customer's business needs.

"Customer needs are very important." Tommy's sales training instructor was always quite adamant about this. "And you need an effective questioning technique to discover them. The wonderful features of your solution are worth nothing, unless they are put in the context of customer needs."

The trainer's big red eyebrows twitched whenever he said this.

And he said it an awful lot.

The 'introductory summary' situation

For his first sales call of the week, Tommy had a meeting with the boss of a large organisation. He had done a good job in arranging this meeting. Or so he kept telling everyone.

"Persistence and charm," he told his sales colleagues, "use plenty of that and you can get past any secretary hell bent on protecting her boss's diary."

Tommy was telling a little white lie with this story, but no matter, no one would care about that when he brought in the big order.

The Two-Minute Message

Actually it was quite a big white lie; the meeting had been agreed during a business luncheon involving the customer executive and Tommy's boss's boss.

Tommy had done lots of homework for this meeting (that was another good point he had picked up from the big man with the bright red eyebrows). He had worked out the questions that he wanted to ask and he had written them down. He had rehearsed them and so he wouldn't need to read from his list.

"Make it a natural conversation, not an interrogation," his tutor had taught him, "once you get the client talking, you can go with the flow."

Tommy arrived early for his appointment. He had allowed himself some time to sit in the reception area and to watch the various comings and goings. He flicked through some of the literature on the reception table and made a few extra notes to his questions.

Tommy smiled to himself. 'Another good tip from my sales training,' he thought.

After they had shaken hands and sat down around the shiny mahogany executive desk, the big Boss man looked across at Tommy.

"OK young man," he said, "why don't you start by telling me what this meeting is all about and what value you think you can offer me".

Tommy was rather taken aback by this statement; the briefing he had got from his manager after the customer luncheon hadn't prepared him for such a blunt opening gambit. He glanced at his notes to remind himself of his first planned question. He knew it anyway, but the notes acted as their usual safety belt.

"You won't need to read your notes," his tutor had told him, "but you'll feel secure having them to hand."

The Two-Minute Message

"Well," Tommy started off, "I wonder if you could tell me about your debt collection process. What are the main problems that you get?"

"All in good time Sonny," the boss man said, "that's a good question and we'll come back to it. But first I need to be happy about your PVC."

Tommy's mind raced, and before he could pretend that he understood, the customer executive continued,

"I'm talking about your purpose, your value and your credibility. Tell me what you can offer me that could give me some benefit, and why *your* company is the one that I should be dealing with."

'Aha,' Tommy thought, `this is now right up my street, I can show him the presentation I've prepared.' Tommy clicked his laptop computer and began to talk about his opening visuals.

"Hold it," the customer boss man interrupted. "You are misunderstanding me. I don't want to see your fancy slides or hear your lengthy sales presentation just yet, I want to hear your two minute summary version."

"Two minute version?" Tommy was puzzled. "I've planned this presentation to last fifteen minutes," he said, "well within our allotted time for this meeting."

"I allowed twenty minutes assuming that this meeting would be a good use of my time," the boss man replied, "I'm very busy so I want to know how this meeting will benefit *me* before I let you start trying to sell me things."

Tommy's mind was racing. He could feel the adrenaline pumping round his system. The customer executive smiled at Tommy.

"Listen son," he said, "think of it as telling me a joke, only I want to know your punchline before you start. Then I will know if it is really

The Two-Minute Message

worth spending some time to hear the whole joke in more detail."

Tommy never got to ask his questions. He flummoxed and he flustered as he tried to make his point succinctly.

The big boss man was very polite. "Well, we've probably got to leave it there for the moment." He looked at his watch.

"Perhaps we can talk about it in more detail another time," he said, "I'll think about what you have told me and I'll be in touch."

But they both knew he didn't really mean it.

TOMMY'S FIRST LESSON

A TMM synopsis is your 'introductory summary'

The Two-Minute Message

The 'elevator challenge'

After a restless night, Tommy is scheduled to make a sales presentation to another important client.

This time he is convinced that everything will turn out OK. Nothing could possibly go wrong. How could it? He had prepared and rehearsed this presentation, but he hadn't learnt it as a script or anything daft like that.

"Make it sound off the cuff," his tutor would say, "even though it won't be."

The sales trainer certainly practised what he preached. Tommy had heard him churn out the same old jokes and anecdotes many times.

Tommy had done his research for this meeting. He knew there would be a dozen people in the audience, and that he had twenty minutes to present his case. He had also been told that the customer people would hold back questions until he had finished his presentation.

"We prefer to hear the whole story before we ask any questions about it." Tommy was delighted when the meeting organiser told him that.

"It's the way that we like to do things round here," she said. "If you stick to your twenty minute slot, it will give us five or ten minutes to ask any questions that we might have."

'Great,' thought Tommy, 'that puts me in control.' His sales training tutor would be pleased.

"Get yourself in control of the questioning process." The sales training tutor would wave his arms around like a windmill whenever he made this point.

The Two-Minute Message

"And then you won't be faced with silly interruptions that can knock you off your stride."

Tommy knew that he had a good case to present. He expected that one or two people would argue with it, but he had anticipated all of the obvious objections and he planned to knock them on the head during his presentation.

He was in good shape. He believed in what he was going to say and that was half the battle.

"Belief is very important," something else the man with the red eyebrows said many times, "if *you* don't look as if you believe in what you are saying then don't expect the audience to get excited. Even if they don't buy from you, they must see you as a sincere businesses person offering sound solutions and advice."

Tommy was pleased with himself. He had worked hard to fix this meeting and he knew that there was a lot of interest in his presentation.

He smiled and nodded to the people as they came into the room and sat down. He chatted to some of them briefly and he introduced himself to others he hadn't met.

"Get comfortable with your audience," his tutor would say, "it is important that both you and they are relaxed. Take any opportunity to speak to them before you start your presentation."

Tommy could see the sense of this. A few words beforehand always help to break the ice and settle the butterflies in the tummy.

Tommy had already made sure that his laptop was plugged in and the projection kit worked well. He was tempted to check it once more, but he settled for a brief shuffle through his note cards.

"Shall we start then?"

The Two-Minute Message

Tommy was startled by the voice from the audience. He looked up at the man who had asked the question.

"Perhaps we should we wait until everyone is here" he replied. The lady boss hadn't turned up yet and Tommy was very keen that she should hear what he had to say.

She was the real decision maker after all.

Tommy looked at his watch. He knew he should have started five minutes ago and he didn't want the audience to get restless.

"Never keep them waiting," his tutor had told him, "your customers are very busy people so you must appreciate the time they have given you. Always make sure that you start on time and that you finish a few minutes early. Your audience will appreciate it"

"Sorry I'm a few minutes late." Tommy was relieved when the lady boss walked in. Now he could stop fiddling with his note cards and get on with his presentation.

"Unfortunately, I can't stay for the presentation." Tommy gulped with dismay when she dropped her bombshell. "But don't worry," she smiled at him, "I know you've put a lot of work into this morning's event and I'm keen to hear your conclusions. Walk me to my car and give me a brief summary."

The lady boss turned to the group, "I'll just borrow him for five minutes then he's all yours," she said, "get yourselves a coffee or tea in the meantime."

As they travelled down in the elevator, the lady boss asked Tommy to summarise his presentation.

Tommy felt lost without his laptop. He had planned his story around his visual aids and he felt helpless without them.

The Two-Minute Message

He flustered and floundered and he started to describe the content of his presentation.

"There's no need to tell me your agenda," she said, "I'm not interested in how you intend to structure your story, I just want a précis of what you will be saying. What's the bottom line of all this work you've been doing?"

The journey was less than a minute but it felt like a lifetime to Tommy. For one crazy minute he considered hitting the emergency alarm and stopping the elevator mid floor. That would give him plenty of time to tell his story; there was so much he could say, but he didn't know where to start.

"I'd planned a twenty minute presentation," he said as they reached the ground floor, "it is very difficult to summarise it in a few words."

The lady boss looked at him. "Well, don't worry," she said, "you get back to the people upstairs, we'd better not keep them waiting. Perhaps I'll try to get the gist of your story from one of them."

The Two-Minute Message

She smiled at Tommy as the doors closed on him. She had pressed the button to send him back upstairs.

Damn, thought Tommy. It wouldn't be problem presenting his case if he was allowed his original allocated time, but one minute! The lady boss would hear a version of his story from someone else, but Tommy knew that he had missed a great opportunity.

He wished he could have crystallised his big presentation into an effective synopsis.

TOMMY'S SECOND LESSON

A TMM synopsis gives you your 'elevator presentation'

The 'set piece' story

Tommy is in a meeting with his boss and some important clients. The clients were passing through town so they had agreed to meet in an airport hotel. It was a couple of hours before the clients had to catch their plane, so they had plenty of time for this meting.

Tommy was delighted that things were now starting to look up. He was getting rather fed up with people wanting him to condense his story - why couldn't they have the courtesy to let him tell it his own way and in his own time?

The customer people were looking rather dazed as Tommy's Boss droned on about the significance of transmission protocols and network speeds.

"So the file sharing process enables the access routines to operate in conjunction with all the network protocols without any default..."

"Sorry, you've lost me there," one of the customer executives chipped in, "what's the relevance of all this technical wizardry and how will it help me?"

Good question thought Tommy. He picked some fragmented mint from the back of his mouth. He had lost the thread of the conversation and couldn't see what his Boss was getting at. He reached across the table for another mint. It always amused him how hotels assumed that business people have an insatiable desire for peppermint and an unquenchable thirst for orange squash and fizzy water.

"Tommy, why don't you take that one, it's more up your field." Gee thanks Boss, thought Tommy swallowing his mint.

"Well," he gulped, "our proposed system is built around self-diagnostic procedures and our service support processes."

The Two-Minute Message

Tommy started to stress the key benefits of his proposals. It wasn't what his Boss had been talking about but it was a critical point to get across.

"Yes, yes, we've heard all that theory," the client managing director interrupted Tommy, "not that I understand it, mind you. And I certainly don't understand what is so special about it."

"Well, the exciting thing is that your people can diagnose a potential problem ahead of time and our remote call centres can talk them though the repair procedures step by step."

Tommy deliberately paused to let the dramatic significance of this point sink in.

"It doesn't even matter what country you could be calling from, because we can funnel the incoming calls to appropriate language skill groups," he went on.

Tommy was enthusiastic about this subject and he knew it very well. "We aim to be the number one service provider in the world," he said.

"We have built this concept into our company mission statement and our training programmes. All of our people now carry a wallet sized card to remind them of this."

The Two-Minute Message

That will show them how serious we are about being a world-class organisation, he thought.

"Well ain't that just bully for you."

Tommy's sixth sense told him that the client's managing director hadn't appreciated the full value of what he had just said.

"No really, this is extremely interesting," Tommy felt compelled to generate an enthusiastic reaction. "We have an on line diagnostic capability built into every one of our systems so each of our seventeen UK service centres can log on to them automatically."

That was the clincher, Tommy thought, now for a bit of icing on the cake, "and by the way," he added, "it's a similar story right across the globe."

"Well it all sounds very Arthur C. Clarke to me."

This wasn't the reaction that Tommy wanted. He had expected the client executive to be more impressed.

"We're a simple organisation," the executive continued, "we aren't technical boffins and we don't need anything as complicated as that."

Tommy was beginning to feel rather frustrated. "Look," he said, "I've got some slides here, I can show you how it all works." He pulled a demonstration binder from his briefcase.

"I think I can help you here."

Tommy looked at the client's technical director. Everyone did. This was a man who rarely spoke but when he did, it always made good sense.

"As we expand," the technical director said, "it is critical that we can guarantee the information flow between the point of sale and our order fulfilment process. Our business depends on it. This flow of information is just as vital to us as the flow of money, so our information systems must be absolutely foolproof."

Everyone nodded and murmured agreement. This was a point that wasn't in any dispute.

"And that's what we get with this new approach," the technical director went on, "the impressive thing about this system is that we don't have to be experts. Fault detection happens automatically, and the number of service centres means that any help we might need is never more than a stone's throw away. I'm all for it."

Tommy was delighted that at least one person in the assembled group had understood the fluency of his argument and could see the sense of it. It was a damned good overview though, better than he had done.

Tommy made a mental note to write it down when he had a spare moment.

TOMMY'S THIRD LESSON

A TMM synopsis gives you your set piece message

The presentation builder

Tommy is planning a thirty-minute presentation for tomorrow's client meeting. He knows the subject very well and he is excited by this great opportunity to impress a senior customer audience.

"Remember that when you present to your client you have a sales opportunity."

Tommy wished that he had a penny for every time the big man with the red eyebrows said this to his students. "You might not be selling a product, " he would say, "but you have a golden chance to sell your personal value and that of your organisation."

Tommy never really understood what the big man meant by the words 'golden chance' but, whatever it was, he wasn't going to let is slip by. It sounded too good to miss.

'If I get the presentation material sorted out quickly,' he thought, 'I'll have plenty of time to plan my script and rehearse until I am fluent.'

Tommy remembered that Charlie had done presentations on this topic so he called him on the telephone. If he could use some of Charlie's material it would give him the time he needed to get his lines worked out.

"Look in my desk drawer," Charlie said, "third drawer down, left hand side. You'll find a couple of presentations I've done in the last three months; they worked very well for me. They're old technology style presentations I'm afraid, I never got the hang of all this fancy computerised stuff, but you should find everything you need in my overhead transparency folder."

Tommy started to convert some of Charlie's ideas into computerised PowerPoint slides. He intended to give the client an unforgettable audio-visual experience.

The Two-Minute Message

"I can pump some life and colour into this material," Tommy muttered as he put the computer software through its paces. Charlie's presentation material contained masses of good information, but the visual aids were as dull as ditchwater. Lists of bullet points to prompt the presenter.

"Remember that the audience members own the visual aids." Tommy now understood the significance of his tutor's statement.

"Think of your visual aids as adding value for the audience members; they reinforce your message. They might also help to keep you on track, but *that isn't their main purpose*. That's what your notes are for."

Tommy was pleased with his first half dozen slides, they were works of art compared to Charlie's original material, but he was aware that time was slipping by.

"Don't keep reinventing the wheel." This was another good point from his sales training tutor. "Learn from your experiences and build on the work that other people have done."

"Hey, what am I doing?" Tommy thought suddenly, "do I really need to create all these slides from scratch?'

The Two-Minute Message

He recalled the presentations that Katrina had done on this topic. They were lively pieces of work and she always seemed to get a good result. Tommy knew that Katrina would have lots of good presentation material set up on her laptop computer. If he could get her material he wouldn't have to spend time translating Charlie's stuff.

Tommy glanced at his watch. It was getting late but it wouldn't be too late to call Katrina. It never was. She was an energetic girl but Tommy reckoned she would have finished greasing her motorbike nipples by now.

"Yes, I've done lots of presentations on that subject," she told him, "stand by and I will email you all my PowerPoint slides."

Hours later Tommy stared at the material he had downloaded and collated together. It was all very good stuff but it seemed as if he had enough content for a two day seminar on the subject. If he flicked through the presentation slides without saying a word Tommy knew that it would take much more time than he had been allowed.

Tommy felt depressed and wondered how on earth he could say all that he wanted to say in only half an hour. There had to be an easier way.

It shouldn't be this difficult to put a presentation together and it shouldn't take this long.

TOMMY'S FOURTH LESSON

A TMM synopsis should be your presentation <u>start</u> point

The Two-Minute Message

The Networking Nightmare

'At last', Tommy thought, 'a real chance to relax and be myself'.

It was one of those networking breakfast meetings. Thirty or forty people eating, chatting and swapping business cards. Tommy was looking forward to standing up and giving his sales pitch.

"You'll get sixty seconds,' his host told him, 'each person stands up in turn and tells the room what he or she can do. It's a great selling opportunity".

Tommy could see people chatting in groups and drinking coffee as they waited for breakfast but he didn't join any conversations. 'I don't want to listen to their sales pitches,' he chuckled to himself, 'I'm the seller here not the buyer. These people are all good targets for my products and services and I'll let them all hear my story at the same time'.

He'd prepared pretty well for this session and he had a cracking pitch. Admittedly, it went on for a bit longer than sixty-seconds, but he'd structured it well; he knew the audience would be impressed by his technical expertise and the benefits of his services.

The Two-Minute Message

He'd looked at the attendance list and spotted some likely candidates for his products and services.

"Try to get the attendee list in advance," his tutor's words made good sense, "you can identify likely clients and say things that will impress them".

Tommy listened as people stood up in turn and spoke about their respective businesses. He was pleased to see that the listeners were nodding and making notes.

He took some business cards as they were passed around. He thought he ought to be seen doing this, although he wasn't really listening to what was being said. Tommy passed a pile of his cards to the person sitting next to him and intimated that these should be circulated.

When his turn came, Tommy stood up with confidence. He'd put every ounce of selling value and benefit into pitch.

"We specialise in ensuring measurable and guaranteed customer delight across all business sectors. We do this in a seamless fashion and with full adherence to defined boundaries and timeframes."

The stunned silence surprised Tommy. Perhaps the audience was overawed by the impact of his initial benefit statement. No one was taking notes; people were looking in his direction with a variety of facial expressions. 'Keep striking while the iron is hot', Tommy thought, 'just wait until they hear the next bit'.

"All of our products are fault-tolerant and the remote fail-safe features kick in after every time the system boots-up. This reliability and serviceability, together our zero-touch self-care architectural framework is the basis for guaranteeing client data integrity."

The overall reaction was more muted than Tommy had hoped for.

The Two-Minute Message

He started to expand on some of his points but the host had signalled that he had run out of time.

"Wow! What a fantastic session," Tommy was pleased when the stranger said this to him as they stood waiting for their coats.

"These breakfasts are great", the stranger continued, "I make lots of good contacts which usually lead to getting some sales – and today has been just like that". The stranger beamed at Tommy. "I'm sorry," he said, "I'm afraid I didn't quite understand what you do but it sounded very good. Perhaps I'll catch up with you next time. Must go".

He waved at Tommy as he dashed towards the door.

Tommy noticed that his business cards were still lying on the breakfast table. He wondered if he should go and pick them up.

He also spotted the stranger, who had been in too much of a hurry to talk to him, chatting happily with other people as if he had all the time in the world.

Tommy was puzzled. He had worked hard on his message and couldn't see why people weren't impressed enough to want to talk to him. Is networking really as difficult as this?

TOMMY'S FIFTH LESSON

Your TMM synopsis gives you your networking message

The Two-Minute Message

The lessons for Tommy (and for all of us)

If the TMM fairy really existed (and who dares say she doesn't?), I wonder what she would say to Tommy. If she were to let him reprise his week 'Groundhog Day' style, what would she ask him to do differently?

She would probably say something along the lines of 'whatever your story, however simple or complex it might be, you need a two minute message for it'. No surprises in that, you might think, given the title of this book.

As a businessman I went to quite a few social and sporting events. These were designed to help business people get to know each other and to do some business 'bonding' - whatever that might mean.

It always surprised me that whenever I asked the 'what does your organisation do?' type of question, it seemed to cause problems or create suspicion. I could see people thinking 'why is he asking that, it's obvious, what's the trick here?'

There was no 'trick' to what I was trying to do. I was just making polite social conversation and it seemed a fair enough question. It gave my hosts the chance to say something memorable and persuasive, and to impress me in some way.

When someone answered my question, more often than not I would get a long and boring answer full of jargon and phrases I couldn't understand. Sometimes (and here's the surprising bit), my host would make some comment about 'not wanting to mix business and pleasure' and change the subject.

This seemed like a lost opportunity, I didn't want to be bombarded with a long sales pitch of course, but a good TMM could have impressed me.

The Two-Minute Message

So you need some good set-piece TMMs about your role and your value.

And that's not just me talking, the TMM fairy says it too.

You need messages in varying levels of detail. Firstly to arouse interest, then to summarise your value and finally, to present your case in detail - a kind of 'message cascade'.

This situation is analogous to good journalism. The headline attracts you to the article; it helps you decide whether or not it'll be worth reading. That's your interest arousing TMM, the top layer of the cascade.

The opening paragraph of the article should give you an overview of what it is about and tell you the angle that the reporter is taking. That's the middle layer.

Finally there is the article itself which should live up to the promise of the previous two layers of the 'cascade'.

Regrettably, I have to tell you that the TMM fairy can't let Tommy reprise his week (she's far too busy elsewhere), but she can help you to learn from Tommy's experiences and avoid the same pitfalls.

She's instructed me to tell you to read on.

5

APPLYING YOUR TMM

Each of Tommy's situations was a significant opportunity: A face to face call on a senior executive, the chance to summarise a business case for the client's CEO, answering a question of detail in a meeting, preparing an important presentation and making good use of networking opportunities.

So let us now examine the main uses of a TMM.

Using a TMM to arouse interest in a new topic

Most sales training courses I attended focused on developing expert questioning techniques and the skill of probing the customer for information. This would help us identify customer issues and problems, and unearth the painful implications of not sorting them out.

We were then taught to show how our solution could remove this pain and give the customer some benefit and value as a result.

That approach is very valid and I'm not knocking it, but as a salesperson, you must be pro-active. You must initiate conversations that add value for the customer and aren't just intended to get information for yourself. It is up to you to identify appropriate topics to discuss.

'Arousing interest' is the main application for a TMM and it is especially valuable when trying to make contact at a senior business level.

The TMM as a 'set-piece' message

In the book 'The Northbound Train', Karl Albrecht describes how a business should have a clear vision of the direction it must take to succeed. He uses the analogy of 'a northbound train' to describe the direction of the business - and its desired speed and momentum.

This analogy can work just as well for a company division, a team or a department.

Wherever you fit, you should know your purpose and your direction, and you should be able to put that over concisely and with passion. Your message should 'position' the role and value of your company (or business function) and entice the audience to want to know more.

Consider what makes your 'Northbound Train' unique. Perhaps it's the speed, or perhaps it's the variety of onboard services. Or maybe it's the ancillary things that customers can pick up along the way.

There are four aspects about your business (or function etc.) that you should know.

1. What you offer (the business you are in and the solutions you offer)
2. To whom you offer it (the nature of your clients)
3. Where you operate (scope, geography, niches, sectors)
4. Your overall purpose (value to the client, value to you)

The answer to each of these points should be full of persuasion and stress your competence and your strengths.

I'm not talking here about set presentations or advertising copy (important though both these things are).

The set piece messages that I have described need to become

The Two-Minute Message

ingrained into our everyday business conversations. We should use them to start debates and to answer questions.

Getting back to the 'Northbound Train' analogy, people might not want to stay on your train for the entire journey, but they should be in no doubt as to its destination, direction and the value of taking a journey with you.

In my work with start up ventures and new initiatives, I ask clients to prepare a 'positioning statement'. This 'core message' is a simple (but not simplistic) summary of what the business does and how the target markets benefit.

'We provide complete preparation and maintenance services for your garden. Every week, every month and every season - all year round support for a fixed monthly fee'.

Statements like these are rarely unique but they are an essential start point for building a good set piece message about your business.

'We provide secure access to private homes for deliveries, service engineers or tradespeople, saving the householder taking time from other critical or preferred activities'

Avoid the clever jargon stuff.

'We provide integrated and architecture frameworks which support real-time, zero-touch self-care systems'

And no, I'm not making it up.

Avoid too the banal generalities that were Tommy's undoing:

'We offer seamless customer experiences that ensure delight'

You will need other 'set piece messages', depending on what you do.

The Two-Minute Message

For example, summaries of your product capabilities, the quality of your customer services, the merits of a particular technology and so on.

Sometimes you will deliver a set-piece message in 'react' mode, i.e. in response to a customer initiative. Other times you could be saying your piece to create a good impression, to provoke a discussion, or to prevent a problem developing.

Mark McCormack, the international sports promoter (sadly no longer with us) insisted that his account executives kept 'accomplishment files.' These were lists of every good thing that the organisation had done for its clients.

In McCormack's line of work, a typical entry would describe a luncheon that he had organised between the client executive and a famous golfer. Or perhaps providing tickets for a major sporting event.

These 'accomplishment files' helped McCormack to remind his customers of the real value that he provided. They were his justification for charging premium prices.

Your challenge is to keep your added value in the forefront of your customer's mind. Over time it becomes 'invisible' and good sales people must work hard to keep it alive and 'visible'.

I had an IBM colleague who was very good at doing this. He could even make a virtue from a problem. "Everyone knows there will be problems from time to time," he told me, "Convincing my customers that we can handle them gives them reassurance in my company".

Every so often, he and his team collated a summary of all the support activities and good-news items that were part of their day to day operations.

"If I use this information wisely," he said, "I can remind the customer executives what they are really getting for their money. It makes them understand what they would lose if they gave their business to a lower cost supplier. My clients aren't buying products from me; they are buying reassurance and peace of mind."

Putting these points across succinctly is what a set piece TMM is all about.

Tommy struggled with his networking message. It isn't easy to summarise what you do in sixty seconds or less.

Have a look at these examples sent to me by 'real' people (Who says Tommy isn't real?)

Some real examples submitted by readers

David Marks Action International
'Behind every great winner is a great coach. Athletes use sports coaches to help them run faster, hit further, jump higher. I help my clients to become the Olympians of the business world. As an ***Action*** *International* business coach, I work with business owners to help them achieve extraordinary results by making manageable changes in their attitude and their activity. My thirty years of business experience and management skills give me the ability to be a practical sounding board, confidant and mentor to business owners'.
(www.action-coaching.co.uk/davidmarks)

Jackie Mitchell, JM Communications
JM Communications is a public relations consultancy, which creates PR campaigns both locally and nationally. Working on behalf of our clients, we build up awareness amongst the target audience, whether it's the end users, business owners or the general public. We place articles, stories and features about your organisation and we can set up radio and TV interviews. We can provide training to help you get

the right messages across in press interviews. All of this ensures that you and your company appear in the media in a very positive light. **(www.jackiem.com)**

Joe Pitts, Managing Director AMBC Ltd
AMBC Ltd was formed in 2002 to offer sales training based on practical experience of the company founders. The business owners (who also deliver the training) apply their sales and account management experiences to produce custom built training perfectly suited to the sales needs of smaller organisations or the more challenging account management requirements of major corporations.
(joe.pitts@btconnect.com)

The TMM as a promotional letter

A TMM is usually a spoken message but it can also be written down. A brief introductory letter can set the scene for an important telephone call or meeting. But it must be brief; preferably no more than a single page.

'Aha,' I hear you say, 'one page - that's easy.' But I'm afraid it isn't; it will take time to do properly. You may know the story about the salesman who said to his customer, "I'm sorry that I wrote you such a long letter, I didn't have time to write a short one".

A succinct TMM letter won't guarantee success, but it will increase your chances.

Almost everybody will read a single page letter in its entirety, but that isn't necessarily the case for something longer. I'm talking here about the 'black-marks-on-white-paper' style of documents. Remember those? But the same argument applies to e-mail correspondence. Get your point across before the recipient has to start scrolling down.

"There are many good reasons for sending a letter ahead of an important call," my old tutor used to say. "It is courteous, it is professional and it brings your name to their attention."

These letters are a form of free advertising. They get put on file and circulated for other people in your customer organisation to see."

In today's email driven world, it can make good sense to write your important TMM letters on your formal, posh paper with your letterhead on display. These documents build a physical record of your value, and your customer is more likely to file a piece of correspondence than an email. Besides, we're all getting a bit bored with email and the clutter that goes with it. A good crisp letter can make an impact.

A neighbour of mine, who worked from home, confirmed my thinking.

"It has suddenly dawned on me," he said, "If my main client contact were to leave, there is very little information about me on the customer files."

He, like most of us, had thrown himself into the convenience and efficiency of email and it's potential anonymity. It probably isn't as anonymous as my friend was worried about, and getting less so, but it is worth regarding some of your good TMM letters as potential brochures.

TMM letters can be difficult to write (hence my earlier quotation about apologising for a long letter), but they are well worth the effort.

Later in this book I'll show a structure that will help you.

Using a TMM to plan a major presentation

The TMM process will also help you to construct the skeleton of an important presentation. One of the main challenges of doing this is deciding what to include in the presentation, and what to leave out. We saw how Tommy decided to take advantage of previous presentation materials. That's fine in principle, but how often have we seen salespeople leafing through old presentation material and shuffling bits of them together to create a new one?

Or more to the point, how often have we done that ourselves?

Every presentation should be built from a two minute version. If you learn nothing else from this book it will have been time well spent for you.

One well known presentation training organisation refers to this kind of synopsis as 'the red thread of the story.' It is the essence of the message.

A good 'red-thread' TMM synopsis will keep you focussed on your presentation objective and it will help you add the necessary amount of detail that you need to achieve it. And no more.

This synopsis will also give you the TMM that you will need to get your client interested in hearing your presentation in the first place. And if you find yourself travelling in an elevator with a senior executive, you will have the presentation synopsis that our young friend Tommy lacked.

So with a good TMM synopsis you can kill two birds with one stone.

Clever eh?

6

BUILDING YOUR TMM

This section of the book gives you a recipe approach to building your two minute message.

It will take time for you to work out the precise words and phrases that you will use, especially if you are preparing a TMM letter, but this step by step approach will help you to get the structure of your message sorted out very quickly.

The 'OATS' principle

This shows the four key stages in building your TMM.

- OBJECTIVE
  State the outcome that you want to achieve
- AUDIENCE
  Identify your targeted person (or persons)
- THEMES
  Select the main points of your message, i.e. the 'themes' that will help you to achieve your objective.
- SYNOPSIS
  Once you've done those three preparatory steps, you then put these themes into the TMM structure. We'll look at that in the next section of this book.

Keep the 'OATS' acronym in mind. It will help you to approach your TMM in the right way.

Defining your 'SMART' objective

In his book, *The Seven habits of Highly Effective People'*, Stephen Covey describes the concept of *'beginning with the end in mind.'* That approach applies to the two minute message process. In other words, your first task is to define the outcome you want from your TMM

A good objective is often referred to as being 'SMART.'

SPECIFIC
It is directed at a specific person (or refers to a specific project).

MEASURABLE
You have defined the end result in such a way that you can 'measure' achievement in a 'yes we have,' or 'no we haven't,' binary sense.

ACHIEVABLE
You can see how the objective can be achieved, given the resources that you have identified.

RELEVANT
The objective makes good sense and is line with your wider goals.

TRACKABLE
You know how you can measure progress towards completing your objective.

'Making a good impression' is a worthy intention, but it doesn't meet our 'SMART' criteria; how would you track it and how would you know when you had achieved it?

If you were setting an objective for a TMM to open your sales call, something like the following statement might be nearer the mark.

'Establish our potential value to the extent that the client is genuinely willing to continue the discussion.'

This is an improvement on the original statement although the phrase *'establish our potential value'* is rather vague, and you would need a more specific focus for your introductory message.

On the positive side, the latter part of the objective statement, *'..the client is genuinely willing to continue the discussion'*, gives a binary measure of success.

You could judge whether or not you had achieved that situation.

TMM objectives versus campaign objectives

When you set an objective for your TMM, you will be doing so in the wider context of your 'sales' campaign (i.e. one where you are trying to persuade your target audience to embark on a course of action).

Don't confuse your TMM objective with the overall objective of your sales campaign. Your campaign, for example, could be to sell a one million pound contract, but winning that contract isn't the objective of your TMM. Your TMM would be intended to arouse the customer's interest in your idea to the extent that he prepared to discuss it with you.

The TMM objective and the campaign objective are related. The TMM is the first milestone point en route to your final goal (your campaign objective).

By the way, if you are able to make a one million pound sale in two minutes, throw this book away and get on with it.

In our example scenario, your TMM objective could be, *'to arouse the client's interest in the potential value of [whatever], and to agree a meeting (involving appropriate parties) where we can discuss this in more detail.'*

At the end of your TMM (and the discussion that follows it) you will have achieved your objective if you could say to your client,

'Thank you for our brief discussion. I will now arrange a session where we can debate this in more detail and we can present our ideas to you. Perhaps a good first step would be for me to suggest an agenda and recommend who we invite to the meeting.'

Or words to that effect – and with less pomposity.

Identifying your target audience

Having established your objective, the next step is to identify the target AUDIENCE for your message.

You would probably have a target audience in mind as you were thinking of your objective, but this process would ruin my OATS mnemonic!

So let us compromise and say that you do them in harmony.

Your target audience could be 'internal customers'. There are other people and functions on whom you are dependent, and to whom you have responsibilities that are not measured in revenue terms. There are times when you will need to engage their attention and persuade them to support you in some way. Your boss, your colleagues and people from other functions in your business, all fall into this category.

Perhaps you want them to support you, or agree to your business plan. Very often you will be trying to persuade them to give you some resources.

You should always plan your TMM for a specific audience, i.e. for a named individual.

It is better, for example, that you design your message for 'Tom Freeman, Marketing Director, Hampton Leisure Limited', than design it for 'any marketing director.'

You could start on a general basis and tailor your message later, I suppose.

But it isn't the best way.

The 'themes' of your message

These are the key points that you want your audience to remember. But you must be selective; saying too much can have a worse effect than saying too little. I'll show you how to structure your message very soon but, first of all, you need to distinguish between possible relevant points of value and random 'facts'.

Don't include 'facts' just because they exist. Be cautious with the chest-beating 'we can do this...' and 'we can do that...' type of stuff.

One client of mine refers to these as Muhammad Ali comments ('I am the greatest') and if you make too many, you could become viewed as being arrogant.

For those of you too young to remember, Muhammad Ali (formerly known as Cassius Clay) used to taunt his opponents in this way.

So be selective when choosing your themes (remember the phrase 'less is more') and make sure that they are relevant to your objective.

Strengths and 'uniques'

You would probably want your TMM to highlight your 'strengths' and the things that make you 'unique'.

But what do these words really mean?

A 'strength' is something that you are good at. It is something that you do (or your organisation does) very well.

Remember though, that there are some basic things that you must have in order to compete in your chosen market sector.

Imagine you were buying a motor car. If the salesman started telling you that the real 'strength' of a particular vehicle was the fact that it had four wheels complete with tyres, you'd think he was crazy. You'd begin to wonder what he had been smoking. These things aren't 'strengths'; they are basic requirements.

The fact that the wheels were of a particular brand of alloy and that the tyres had the latest super-grip capability to keep you secure in wet conditions, might be factors worth highlighting.

A 'strength' is something beyond the basic requirements that make your product 'fit for purpose'. It is something worth featuring because it adds credence to your claim.

A 'unique' is something that only you can offer, or something that you are best at doing.

The Two-Minute Message

Let me give you an important phrase to keep in the back of your mind whenever you try to identify your 'strengths'. Better still, I suggest you write in your diary, enter it in your filofax, put it on your PDA or key it into your laptop.

I've got it scratched on my Elvis Presley pencil box. Here it is,

'A *'strength' is only a 'strength' if we can exploit it to achieve our objective.*'

This will help you filter out some 'strengths' which could be genuine statements of truth, but which are not relevant to your current TMM.

Ask yourself the question, 'could we exploit this (feature) to make our campaign objective more attainable?'

Likewise a 'weakness' is only relevant if it genuinely inhibits your progress.

So let us assume that you are clear about the topic you want to discuss and that you have a target audience in mind. You know the outcome that you want and you have sorted out a list of the main points that you want to make.

You are now ready to construct your TMM.

7

THE TMM FOUR PART STRUCTURE

This is the 'S' bit of the 'OATS' acronym; creating the 'synopsis'. In other words, putting the components together to construct your TMM.

A TMM has four components, constructed in the following sequence:

1. The audience context statement
2. Your key theme
3. Your supporting themes
4. Your closing statement

This section of the book will explain each of these elements and give you some examples.

However, please remember my comments about the 'long letter' and the 'short letter'. Writing a good TMM takes time. It isn't easy (at first).

Actually it's never easy - but it gets easier with practise.

Your audience context statement (ACS)

Every statement of value must be set in an audience context. That should be obvious but I'll repeat it with some emphasis,

The Two-Minute Message

'Every statement of value must be set in an audience context'

Excuse me for a moment while I scratch it on my pencil box.
The opening statement of your TMM (your ACS) should state something that is relevant to the recipient of the message. It should *not* say anything about you, your company or your products.

The same rule applies to a written TMM. Your opening sentence, or paragraph, should set the scene for your message in customer terms.

In both of these instances (a spoken or written TMM), I'm talking about situations where you are initiating the conversation and trying to arouse interest in your topic. If you are answering a direct question, the context could be self-evident but, even then, a brief context statement will make your message more relevant.

A good ACS will state an accepted (or likely) customer issue or business statement of fact, and its implications. It should be a statement that the recipient would agree to.

- *'We are aware of your plans to ...'*
- *'In your line of business, Mr Customer, we have noticed that other organisations are reviewing the issue of ...'*
- *'The recent business articles on (something or other) point out that ......*
- *'Businesses like yours Mr Customer, are facing the challenges of expanding abroad into to new market areas ....'*
- *'Success in your marketplace depends on the quality of service that you give your customers and how well you can satisfy their demands ...'*
- *'Many of our clients tell us that one of the biggest issues today is ....'*
- *'The educational challenges today are greater than they have ever been...'*

You can also make your ACS thoughtful and reflective.

'It occurs to me that one of the great opportunities in your line of work is......'

Your context statement doesn't have to be earth shattering; you aren't trying to AMAZE your target audience - save that for when you sell your value – you are setting the CONTEXT for your proposition. Remember my 'seven seas' rule.

Here some statements taken from real life. You don't need to know the organisations (although you might guess their respective lines of business).

'In an attempt to satisfy the world's increasing demands for energy, it's easy for companies to overlook the importance of plants and animals. But ignoring endangered species can be very costly. Lasting environmental damage and public outrage are the real business consequences of forgetting the small and the vulnerable'

No one can really disagree with that. It shouts out 'we are an energy company that cares'. I would add the word 'justifiable; in front of 'public outrage' to give it more impact, but they didn't ask my opinion.

That's their loss.

Look at this next one. It sets the scene by making a statement about technology.

'New technologies have given rise to unprecedented possibilities in every aspect of our lives. The application of these technologies to the HR function is leading to radical changes in the way in which this function is performed'

You could replace 'HR' in that statement with the name of almost any business function and the statement would be applicable.

Here's another.

'Every organisation has the problem of lost time, productivity and customer support due to employees taking time off for mundane but necessary home activities – such as trade deliveries or service engineer visits. This creates stress for employees as they decide whether to take time off, arrange 'informal cover' or rearranging working life to suit – with no guarantees that the commitment will be met...'

The Two-Minute Message

The opening statement is very important. It creates the context for your message and makes it more valuable and relevant. Advertising companies write in this way instinctively.

Your opening statement should be non-contentious (ideally) and one that your audience will accept readily, so there is no need for you to labour this part of your message. An audience context statement will set the scene for your 'value propositions' or whatever terminology you use to describe how wonderful you can be.

And it will make one hell of a difference.

Trust me, I'm a doctor.

Your Key Theme

This is the heart of your message. It must be CLEAR and CONCISE. And it should relate to the CONTEXT you set up in your ACS.

It will reflect what your business does (relevant to the audience context) and is a statement of your value.

'We link your loan and savings accounts thereby guaranteeing reduced interest payments, whilst letting you retain control over your individual accounts.

'We provide a full range of outsourced IT services and capabilities that will support all your current and emerging business requirements'

'Our application can run on any technology platform and, using the Internet, can transfer between platforms to suit your requirements'

'We have an agency and support network in every European country which we co-ordinate from our head office'

The Two-Minute Message

'We guarantee door to door delivery within 24 hours. No delays, no excuses, just your package where you want it'

'We help organisations to develop their business strategies and to build the value stories and client engagement skills to implement them'

'The Two Minute Message™ process will help you to sell your value. It will help you build your client relationships and give you increased revenues as a result.'

You don't select your key theme at random, nor do you choose the most impressive item from your list of possible options.

Your key theme should be the one that will help you to make the most progress towards achieving your objective. And it should be a logical extension of your audience context statement.

For example, consider a message that starts as follows:

'We have read about your ambitious plans to expand your business into to Europe and the demands that this will place on the local operations in each country.'

Given that ACS, your key theme should cite the main feature of your approach that could help the customer to do this.

'We have full support operations in each of these countries which we can co-ordinate from the UK. No one else can offer this level of support.......'

Now I don't know if that point is any good or not, it's an academic example (actually it isn't, but I've neutralised it to protect the innocent). But it is a *relevant* theme; it addresses the issue raised in the audience context statement.

A different key theme could be less effective.

The Two-Minute Message

'We invest sixteen million pounds a year in research and development.'

That impressive statement might be true but it doesn't build on the audience context statement quoted earlier. It is a 'Muhammad Ali' claim, made in isolation.

So there are two questions you should ask about your key theme. There are two tests that you should apply to verify that you have chosen the most appropriate theme to spearhead your message.

1. Does this theme relate to my audience context statement? Does it address the issue or implications that are contained within it?

2. If I lead with this theme, will it help me to achieve my objective?

Why only a single theme?

A fair question - after all, there are many points that you probably could make. I'm often asked that question on my TMM workshop sessions.

'Tell me, oh Great One,' a participant will say, 'I have two very good points that I want to make, why can't I use them both?'

It can be difficult to select a single theme, I grant you, and it isn't a disaster if you are unable to pick a main one, but it is an excellent discipline to try to do so. It forces you to tailor the message to your audience and to be crystal clear about your objective.

Nine times out of ten when my workshop participants struggle to identify a single key theme, it is because either they are not clear about their objective or they haven't got a specific audience in mind.

But we sort it out in the end. Usually.

The Two-Minute Message

Think of it as like having a set of bow and arrows. You have an arrow firing mechanism and you have a loaded quiver to select from.

These arrows represent your possible 'themes'.

In this analogy all your themes are the same, so let's take it a stage further and imagine they are all different. Different sizes, different flights, different capabilities.

Some of these arrows are designed to kill, some to send messages, some to light beacons and so on.

Depending on your target (target audience) and what you are trying to do (your objective), you need to select the most appropriate arrow to fire first.

This is analogous to selecting your key theme. It is very important to pick the correct one – the one that best suits the situation ('context').

Your 'Supporting Themes'

Remember the old song, 'it ain't what you do, it's the way that you do it'. Most businesses fall into that category.
Your 'Key Theme' may be stating something that other people could claim equally. Your supporting themes prove your CAPABILITY and CREDIBILITY (two of the 7 'C's) and show what makes you special.

They show your uniqueness.

There are two types of supporting theme.

The first type adds credence to your key theme by providing supporting evidence to substantiate it. Client references are a good example of this type. If your key theme describes a feature of your product or service which can help your clients get new routes to market, a good supporting theme would be to comment on the number and types of business that are realising these benefits. Putting some proof in the pudding, so to speak.

You get credence by quoting specific names, 'we did this for client XYZ and they saved ....'. Don't forget too what you have done within your own organisation. Some people say that internal references add less impact than those that are client based. That's debatable but, in any case, don't underrate their value.

There will also be some valid themes which are unrelated to the key theme, but which could help the client to address the implied issues of the audience context statement. That's the second category of supporting theme.

We can usually find a home for some of our rejected key theme contenders in the 'supporting themes' category.

Your Closing Statement

This statement should make a link back to your objective by making an appropriate suggestion or request. This gets you the 'commitment' you seek.

'So you see Mr Customer, there are several areas where we could help you cut costs. Can I suggest that we do some more work on this and present our findings to you?'

That is OK, but it could be strengthened. We might have let ourselves in for quite a bit of work without any real commitment from the customer. It can be easy for a customer to say 'yes' to your suggestion out of courtesy (or a desire to close the meeting!).

You can test the customer's commitment by asking for a further meeting and agreeing the agenda. Or by asking him/her to agree that you work alongside some customer staff to do your preparatory work.

If you are giving a set piece TMM in response to a question, you might feel that there isn't a need for much of a closing statement.

Possibly so, but for each of your set pieces, think of the next logical steps.

Is there a workshop or a seminar that you are running that could give your clients more information on the topic?

Are there people in your organisation who have the same business challenges as your client? Get the two people together for some good old 'shared-learning'.

Are there news articles or other pieces of literature that you could refer them to?

The Two-Minute Message

Finally, remember this GOLDEN RULE when preparing your TMM.

Write your TMM as if you are going to send it as a letter. Even if you're planning it as a telephone call or presentation. Write it on a single page.
And I mean one page of normal text size!

> Don't play silly games to cram in as many words as you can into the smallest possible space!

One page will allow you about 300 words or so.

Even if you are planning a face to face sales meeting, writing your TMM is a good discipline. It will help you to sort out the words and phrases.

You are writing your TMM to make is as squeaky-clean as you can. You are NOT doing it to learn a script or to be able to recite your message parrot-like.

The Two-Minute Message

8

YOUR RANGE OF TMM TOPICS

There will be some topics that you would like to discuss with your customers, and there will be others that you could expect to be asked about. In every case you should try to sell your TOTAL VALUE.

On our value building workshops I make the analogy of a triple flavoured ice cream cone. Think of a hot summer afternoon and the pleasure of clutching one of those triple cones with dollops of vanilla, strawberry and chocolate-chip ice cream. These three flavours represent your three key strands of possible value.

The Three Flavours of Value

- PRODUCTS AND SOLUTIONS VALUE: This is the vanilla stuff; the net benefits that your customer will get from your products and services. Typical benefits are reduced costs, increased efficiency, improved routes to market and so on. The customer gets value when the benefits exceed the costs of ownership.

  This should be familiar territory for all sales people so I'll say no more about this aspect.

- ORGANISATIONAL VALUE: Your customer could be facing business issues that your organisation understands very well. If your business has been successful in expanding abroad, downsizing, introducing home-working or whatever, you can apply that knowledge to your customer. As a consultant, I charge for such services but your 'company knowledge' could be part of the added-value of doing business with you. Come to think of it, it might be a damned good reason for the customer to want a relationship with you, even when he isn't in a buying mood.

  Your customer base is another asset you could exploit. You know how other businesses and market sectors tackle particular problems and, without breaking confidences, you could apply that knowledge.

  This is adding a strawberry flavour of value to the vanilla.

  Think of your company 'R.I.S.K.' – i.e.. areas of value you can exploit from your company 'Resources, Information, Skills and Knowledge'

PERSONAL VALUE: Chocolate-chip ice cream is the clincher for me; it's that little extra touch that sways the balance and convinces me to buy. Your personal background, experiences and business contacts could add value to your customer's strategic debate. Think about your job role and those of your supporting team members. What would the customer lose if these roles didn't exist? Conversely, what potential value do they add?

If you focus purely on solutions value, you could get dragged into a price debate. That's fine if you are a vanilla flavoured value business only.

Very often the real added value sits outside the context of a specific proposition – this is your 'enduring compelling value' (ECV).

If you are in the added-value arena make sure that you sell your total value. You don't have to fill all three cones equally, but don't expect to win if you leave any of them empty.

Good tip that. I'll need to get another pencil box.

TMM topic examples

Here are some examples from my TMM workshops. They might not set you on fire, but remember these are just working titles to get us started. They can be jazzed up later.

PRODUCTS AND SOLUTIONS VALUE
- *'The unique benefit of (a particular product)'*
- *'How our solution improves your route to market'*
- *'The benefits that (another client) gets from our products and services'*
- *'How our offerings complement your current supplier's products'*
- *'The saving that you'll get from our proposed solution'*
- *'How we give you competitive advantage'*

ORGANISATIONAL VALUE
- *'Our company vision and its relevance to our clients'*
- *'How our experience and knowledge (in a particular area) can help you'*
- *'The relevance of our investments in research and development'*
- *'Our policies regarding joint ventures and partnership arrangements'*
- *'Our value in helping you cope with business change'*

PERSONAL VALUE
- *'My job function and how it can benefit your business'*
- *'The value of my background skills and experience (my CV)'*
- *'The added value you will get from our support resources'*
- *'The rationale of our latest reorganisation (and how this benefits our clients)'*
- *'The value of our specialist skills and functions'*

You will notice that the phrasing of many of these topic titles implies a benefit. Delivering an effective two minute message is much more than making a succinct statement to answer a question, or to state a case. It should be phrased to arouse interest, and to sell the benefit of yourself, your company and the services you offer. Possibly all three.

9

THE FIVE KEY MESSAGES YOU WILL NEED

The five key messages are:

1. Your Core Function and Purpose TMM
2. Your Interest Arousing TMM(s)
3. Your 'ECV' TMM
4. Your Business Strapline
5. Your Internal TMM

Competing in a commercial world isn't easy but without these five key messages it can be impossible.

If you want feedback on your 5KM, or you'd like a workshop to help you write them, please let me know.

1. <u>Your Core Function and Purpose TMM:</u>
   This is a clear, direct statement describing what you do. It is rarely unique and is often the core of other messages.

   Before you think about value propositions and other stories to drive your clients and colleagues into a motivational frenzy, write down your 'core function and purpose'. We covered this earlier in the book. Summarise what you 'do' - but do so without using any adjectives or adjectival phrases. Be clear about what you are, and what you are not. Focus on something that differentiates you from your competition.
   'We provide engineering support and maintenance services for all makes of personal computer. No job is too small, no machine is too old'

2. **Your 'Interest Arousing' TMM(s):**
   These are your C7 TMMs designed to arouse client interest in specific topics. Use these to show your 'thought leadership'. This isn't necessarily creating some new 'gee whiz' idea that's no-one has ever thought of, it's about being proactive. Your topic range should be more than specific sales propositions; develop a message to sell your personal or organisational value.

3. **Your 'ECV' TMM:**
   One of your messages should describe your 'enduring compelling value'. Your 'ECV' message will feature the topics identified in your 'strawberry' flavoured section of the ice-cream cone. This message describes aspects about you that are compelling & which sit outside the context of any specific proposition. These value elements are always there – come rain or shine.

4. **Your Business Strapline:**
   This phrase or statement encapsulates your purpose and value in fifteen words or less. You should have one of these even if your business doesn't have an official strapline. This is your 'two second message'.

5. **Your Internal TMM:**
   The 'Wow, so this is us!' message. It's a summary of your culture, ethos and style that will motivate your colleagues and employees. It's the message that will make people want to work with you – and keep those that do.

Building your C7 Internal TMM – an example

The purpose of this is to get you and your colleagues COMMITTED to your way of working and enthusiastic about what you do. This message will give a flavour of your culture; they 'way you do things'

The Two-Minute Message

Here's a TMM targeting the employees of an IT solutions provider. The aim is to give them a clear message on what the business is all about and to be clear about how it could affect their job functions. It's also intended to motivate them. This is (PART OF) an internal message and therefore confidential to the company concerned. So I've neutralised it.

We live in a business world of unprecedented change. The speed of Internet development and the deregulation of business boundaries create opportunities for every business to exploit new markets, to enter new geographical areas and to develop new routes to market.

This dynamic business environment places inexhaustible demands an organisation's ability to maintain the levels of ICT skill and infrastructure to support its business needs.

We help the senior management of a business to understand this changing environment and to assess the implications on their IT operations. We provide a range of outsourced IT solutions that will support our customers' current and emerging business requirements.

Our solutions go beyond mere support: We offer measurable business value and guaranteed levels of performance that are second to none and we have an extensive client base that would be happy to support our claims.

This environment provides exciting, rewarding and challenging career opportunities for our employees and business partners.
We work in a very innovative and stimulating environment and we work very hard to balance the needs and aspirations of our employees with the demands of our workplace. In order to satisfy client demands, we need a flexible workforce in terms of skill development, working hours and working location. Our policy is to attract and retain the best people in our industry and to motivate and reward them accordingly. (Evidence of this...)

What words come to mind about this company's 'brand image'? Innovative, dynamic, leading-edge?

And it's 'culture'?

Demanding, rewarding, flexible?

Possibly.

That example followed my TMM structure.

Context: Setting the right background for your value / positioning statement.

Key Theme: This your core approach. Look at your CORE purpose that you defined earlier and your mission statement (if you have one). This should address the need stated or implied in the context.

Supporting Evidence / Supporting Themes
What makes you credible and good at what you do?
How can you show your seriousness of intent?
What are your strengths / unique selling points?
What are the benefits of working for you?
What evidence do you have to support that?

10

YOUR BRAND, IMAGE AND CULTURE

Definitions

These are my definitions; they don't come from a dictionary or business bible. They work for me, I hope they do for you too.

BRAND is 'an indication of the value that the customer can expect'.

Tom Peters talks about today's 'new brand world'. Everything is branded. Branding creates loyalty. It's the factor that makes each of us think, 'I know what to expect – and I like it'.

So the purpose of your 'brand' is to create pleasant expectations in your clients' minds and to generate their loyalty.

IMAGE is 'how you are seen by the outside world'. In my book (and this is my book) it means the same thing as brand. You want your clients to have a positive 'image' of your company.

A consistent positive image becomes your 'brand'.

When you think of an organisation or you see its logo, you get an impression.

A 'brand' has established itself when the mere sight of a simple logo gives you a good feeling about that organisation and the value you can expect every time you deal with it.

The Two-Minute Message

This value will be consistent (therefore you <u>expect</u> to get it) and it can be in terms of price, quality, comfort, style, whatever.

Gurus tell us that 'experience comes before the brand'. Your 'brand image' emerges from the sum total of the customer experiences that you give.

- How do you want your customers to describe your brand?
- What words would your customers use when they see your name or logo? – Steady now!
- How does that compare with how <u>you want</u> your customers to describe you?

CULTURE is how your organisation operates internally. It's your internal style. This is how you do things. Whether or not you think you have a 'culture', you do. There is a 'truth' about how you operate – and how you are perceived by outsiders.

Consider what words and adjectives describe the style and modus operandi of your organisation / department. Write them down, but be honest. My first English teacher referred to these as 'truthful describing words'.

Your internal culture and your external brand image are related and must be in harmony.

Creating your 'Strapline'

A 'strapline' is a condensed message. In a single line, it tries to encapsulate your brand value. You often see them below the logo or title of a company.

Even if you don't like the idea of promoting a single line message, I recommend that you create a 'virtual strapline'. It will focus your mind on what you do, how you operate and the value you give.

The Two-Minute Message

Put it on your business card – and be proud to show it.

This doesn't just have to be at company level by the way; you can have a 'virtual strapline' for your function, department or role.

It can do all three things if you make it. But it doesn't have to; you might just want to create an identifiable brand slogan.

Just do it' means Nike to everybody.

In fact the Nike swooshing tick (taken from the Greek goddess Nike) conveys an entire brand. I'm not sure what they are asking me to 'do' – but it feels stylish.

One of my straplines is *'helping clients to sell their value'*

It sums up my core activity.

Everything I do is to that end, so I want people to know that. All of my workshops and support activities are linked to helping clients achieve an end goal.

Straplines can be used in a variety of ways:

- Sum up the core activity or value proposition

The Two-Minute Message

'bringing passion to sales performances'
'business and management development'
'creating stakeholder wealth'
'empowering people through great software, any time, any place, any device'
'helping small business succeed on line'
'helping individuals and organisations to achieve their goals'
'providing real world solutions for the work that you do'
'active support for business'
'supporting your ICT infrastructure'
'for training as unique as you are'
'anytime, anywhere communications'
'bringing traffic to your website'
'for access to global talent'
'never knowingly undersold'
'taking the complexity from IT'
'there when you can't be'
'providing safe and fairly priced accommodation via responsible landlords'

- Create an identifiable brand slogan that sets a picture in our minds whenever we see it
'just do it'
'it's the feeling inside'
'innovation delivered'
'it's better to be there'
'our challenge is life'
'answers for questions yet to come'
'everywhere you look'
'we weren't born with our reputation, we've earned it'
'doing the unthinkable'
'where business relationships begin'
'the power to make YOU different'

Many of these could be improved of course, but each of them makes a statement.

Each one tries to present a 'viral message;' about the person or organisation it represents.

11

VIRAL MARKETING

The TMM technique works on the principle of 'interruption marketing'. You force yourself on people and, in the nicest possible way, get their attention and engaging their interest. You do the work. You are proactive. You get them thinking about something 'new' – you are the thought leader.

In his book 'UNLEASH YOUR IDEA VIRUS', Seth Godin defined the concept of 'viral marketing'.

This is where your marketplace latches on to your idea and, consciously or unconsciously, the people in your marketplace spread your message. The process is analogous to how the common cold virus gets about, hence the phrase 'viral marketing'.

In Godin's book, he describes how people become 'sneezers' and pick up catchphrases and other identifiers to spread a message.

Hotmail grew to 10 million users without the effort (and expense) of a major advertising campaign. Every email message carries an advertisement for Hotmail as part of the signature. Every Hotmail user becomes a 'sneezer' and helps to spread the 'hotmail virus'. Every recipient picks it up and becomes a possible 'sneezer', passing it on.

Whatever concept you are trying to put over, identify your 'sneezing' mechanisms and exploit them.

Your viral marketing mechanisms

Think about all the ways you could spread your message like a virus.

Here are some possibilities:

- Develop a repeatable story about what you do and the value that you give. This is a C7 TMM highlighting your value. How could you get your clients to spread your message of value? What would encourage them to do this for you? Some networking organisations advise that you create a 'memory hook'; something that makes people think about you and what you offer.

- Write a strapline or catchphrase that sums up your core purpose, role or value. Put this message on your business card and your other collateral. Use it as your email signature.

    William Freeman
    CAMBRIDGE ASSOCIATES
    Creator of the Two Minute Message™ Technique
    The PROVEN way to sell your value
    www.TwoMinuteMessage.com

- Consider how you could you get 'your value phrase' into people's psyche – and linked to you. Remember that your value or uniqueness isn't just about what you do, it's how you do it.

- We all know the Nike 'tick' but it isn't easy to create a similar viral picture about our businesses. Is there a picture, logo or colour that suits you?

- Investigate regular communication mechanisms and events: a client forum, business networking sessions, shared-learning seminars, regular e-newsletters.

- Produce press releases and business articles that promote your expertise. Offer the articles for no fee in return for a 'sidebar' giving your contact details.

- Implement a 'formal' referral programme where your customers promote your services in return for a fee. Which reminds me..... please ask me how you can make money referring my TMM services.

Getting the words right

A local (to me) management resources company (called Transition) has the strapline

'The people business for business people'

It has a nice palindromic ring to it. It's a more memorable phrase than,

'We are human resource consultants offering services to business people and their organisations'

So pick your words carefully. Make them memorable so that whenever they are seen or heard, your company name or idea comes to mind. If these words become unique to you, then so much the better.

'Is that your final answer?'

The TV programme 'Who wants to be a Millionaire' uses that phrase for legal reasons, but it is now its unique catch phrase. The phrase is legally necessary so that there can be no doubt that the contestant has finished 'thinking aloud' and is giving a formal answer. But it's turned into a memorable catchphrase identified with the programme.

Look at your strapline and see how you can make a memorable phrase from it. Then consider how you're going to promote the phrase to your marketplace.

'Excite your Customers with a Two Minute Message™*'*

That's one of my catchphrases. I need a better one though. Any suggestions?

SAGE example

Here's a recent SAGE advert. It shows how the strapline and the value message link together. The strapline reads, *'active support for business'*

This doesn't tell you anything about Sage products but it gives a flavour of what it does. They also use the longer strapline, *'our software will transform your business'.* So, if you didn't already know, this tells you they are in the software business.

The full advert reads:

As a growing business, you're probably using a number of different software packages. But are they really working together to cut costs, save time and improve customer service?

For example: Can you transfer your payroll details into your accounting software with one single posting? Or automatically download the orders you receive on your webshop? Can your salesforce access a customer's financial history directly from their contact management software?

If so, chances are you're already one of the 40,000 businesses in the UK who are using Sage software.

Sage has a range of software for all sizes of businesses, from start-ups to large enterprises.

The Two-Minute Message

So as your business grows, your Sage system can grow with you. Our software packages are designed to integrate with one another so they won't just help run your business.

They will help you transform the way you do business.

140 words. Not bad.

It isn't an exact replica of my TMM format but the first part of the advert sets the context.

The comment about 40,000 customers gives comfort and credibility. The point about integrated packages and their ability to handle business growth is well made.

I don't know if any aspect of this message is unique but it tells a good story.

It could be made into a decent TMM (anyone from Sage out there?).

12

FROM TMM TO PRESENTATION

Your TMM will help you to gain the attention of your target audience. It will get you the 'air time' to tell your longer story.

Once you've gained commitment to the next step, you'll often find yourself having to give a full sales pitch - a compelling and persuasive (same thing!) presentation.

Here's a flow of ideas I've taken from a well-known classical story.

No prizes for guessing it correctly.

- baby boy is abandoned to grow up in the orphanage workhouse
- he questions the strict regime and, in anger, he is offered for sale
- his employer is strict and very cruel so the boy runs away
- he meets a criminal gang of boys who befriend him
- against his will he gets involved in a theft
- his victim is a good and rich man, who takes pity on the boy
- the rich man befriends the boy and takes him into his family
- the criminal gang are afraid that the boy will betray them and they plot to recapture him from the rich benefactor
- the criminal gang capture the boy
- they find out that he was abandoned by a young, dying mother and that he has wealth that he could claim
- a member of the gang tries to help the boy escape
- she is murdered by one of the gang leaders
- the police pursue the gang and arrest them
- the boy inherits his birthright and is adopted by his rich benefactor

Many story book writers use this approach to get the flow of ideas in place and then develop the compelling story. I can't say for certain that Charles Dickens used it to write 'Oliver Twist', but Lionel Bart used something like it to write his musical, *'Oliver'*

A storyboard is a flow of ideas.

A TMM outline is such a storyboard - and it's a great way to build a presentation. It's the only way.

Template for a 'persuasive presentation'

Most persuasive / sales presentations can fit into the six step format model shown below.

It's an extension of the TMM model.

Build your outline ideas in this format (a bit like Lionel Bart did for 'Oliver') and then add detail to the level you need. And no more.

1. SET THE SCENE

2. SET THE CONTEXT (Audience Context)

3. STATE YOUR MAIN POINT (Key Theme)

4. PROVE YOUR CREDIBILITY & JUSTIFICATION (Supporting Themes)

5. PROPOSE ACTIONS (Close)

6. SUMMARISE AND CLOSE (Close in context)

Presentation Format – example

SET THE SCENE
This is not part of your presentation. Try to do the 'good morning, nice to see you', handshaking introductory stuff before you start your formal presentation.

If you have the chance to introduce yourself by name to each member of the audience before your formal presentation, do so. It'll blow the cobwebs from your vocal chords. 'Speak informally before you speak formally'

If you are forced to include personal introductions as part of your formal presentation, keep them very brief – and outside the 'formal' bit of your presentation.

SET THE CONTEXT (Audience Context)
This is the start of your formal presentation. This section is audience context oriented - lots of *'you'* in the spoken word, very little *'we'*.

- The 'challenge or issue' they (the audience members) face. Be bold and honest about the 'problem' as you see it.
- How you know that (but only if necessary to tell them)
- The (quantified) benefits of resolving this issue and the impact of not doing so
- The urgency / timescales (to audience for getting these benefits)
- The purpose of your presentation (' to show how the benefits can be achieved')
- Presentation 'signposts' (the agenda - although not necessarily a formal one)

STATE YOUR MAIN POINT / PROPOSAL (Key Theme)
- Your 'core' proposition: A clear, succinct and bold statement of what you propose to do, by when and by what means
- The value and benefit that will result

PROVE YOUR CREDIBILITY (Supporting Themes)
- Your approach to the problem (factors that maximise opportunity and minimise risk); the 'making-it-happen' plan
- Your track record (internal and external) that gives credence to your proposition
- Relevant skills, knowledge and other 'asset' values of your organisation (including associates and partners, if appropriate)
- Factors that make you unique

PROPOSE ACTIONS (Close)
- The next steps (what you want target audience to DO)
- Clear summary of resources and commitments you need

SUMMARY & CLOSE (Close in context)
- [Hosted discussion for agreed time period – if necessary]
- '30 second' TMM summary
- Ask for what you want
- I'll repeat that – Ask for what you want

The Presentation Close

This is worth a few special comments.

The last thing you say is likely to stick in the minds of your audience more than anything else, so prepare it well.

Make your finale a cracking TMM than encapsulates your entire presentation.

Imagine the CEO of your client turns up *just to listen to your closing remarks*.

I'll pause for a moment while you scratch that tip on your pencil box.

The 'OATS for Vitality' model for building a presentation

The acronym refers to the six key steps to building a presentation.

OBJECTIVE
- Define the purpose of your presentation and the outcome you want. Be clear about what you want your audience to agree to and what you want them to DO.
- Write this down so it is clear and unambiguous

AUDIENCE
- Identify the target audience for your proposition
- Identify them by function and / or name

THEMES
- Identify all the different components of your presentation ('jig-saw pieces')
- Write down the titles of each component ('customer issues', 'costs', risk factors', 'quantified benefits', 'our solution'.... etc. Imagine you are labelling each jig-saw piece to say what it is (not where it goes)

SEQUENCE
- Put the pieces in the right order (build your storyboard)
- Use the TMM structure to help you
- Make sure you have a proper 'close' component

FLESH-OUT
- Add the minimum (repeat *minimum*) necessary amount of detail to each element to achieve the desired objective
- Resist the temptation to add excess detail. Hold back.

VISUALISE
- Plan the visual (and hand-out) material

Learn from the Theatre

There are many opinions about the 'right' attitude to presentations, but here are a couple of good theatrical analogies.

If you want a good format for your next sales presentation, think 'Lieutenant Colombo'. Most people will know of this TV detective character developed by the actor Peter Falk, who portrays him brilliantly.

All the 'Colombo' stories have the same structure and plot formula.

At the beginning, we see a crime being committed (usually a murder) and the thing that makes compulsive viewing is then watching and waiting to see how Colombo manages to nail the criminal.

This 'Colombo' structure is similar to that of a sales presentation. The nature of the proposition is made at the start (we know who 'did it') so there's no mystery about the proposed conclusions. The real purpose of the presentation is to present the argument and detail needed to justify the proposition.

This is very different to a normal detective story, which gradually evolves and keeps you in suspense until the final cliff-hanging page.

There's nothing to stop you presenting your compelling case in that way, but you run the risk of running out of time before you reach a conclusion – or losing audience interest along the way. Chances are too that you'd hit a few diversions and detailed side conversations that interrupt your flow.

So copy the Colombo format for your next important presentation.

The Two-Minute Message

Practise is important too (note the 's' spelling, in this instance it's a verb not a noun).

Most people would agree that the Royal Shakespeare company will give a better performance of 'Hamlet' than the local amateur dramatic society, despite the fact that both groups are using the same story and the same words (most of the time).

That's partly due to the ability, the training and the experience of the performers and the time they take to practise (there's that 's' word again), or 'rehearse' if we use correct theatre parlance.

A theatrical company takes about two weeks (full time) to rehearse a three hour play. And that doesn't include time spent creating the text, the author has done that. Nor is it spent plotting the moves, the director will have done that beforehand.

That's a thirty-to-one ratio for rehearsal time versus performance time.

Admittedly a lot of theatrical complexity comes from the number of actors involved (and probably some of their moods and tantrums), but play these numbers how you like, the point is the same.

Once you have built your compelling story there is no substitute for practise, practise and even more practise.

The 'over-rehearsal' myth

I'll keep this section brief. There isn't such a problem. You can't over-rehearse. You can't spend too much time becoming clear and comfortable with your story and getting confident about putting it across.

What you can do, however, is get tired and become complacent. Your energy level can drop.

It's exactly the same for professional actors saying the same lines night after night. They know the play backwards (and forwards too we hope). Like them, you need to be fresh for every performance and force yourself to make that freshness show.

But don't confuse problems of tiredness with over-rehearsal.

13
TAKING THINGS FORWARD

You might have read this book from cover to cover in a single sitting.

That's what I intended.

Maybe you paused along the way to make some notes or to identify some TMM topics that are relevant to your business situation. That's the first step. If you haven't already done it, skim through again and make your notes as you go along.

In the appendix you will see a blank template to help you write your two minute message. I like this document not just because I created it, but because it is simple and there isn't much space in which to write (unless you expand it to A1 size). Use this document to sort out the substance and flow of your message. You can finalise your precise wording afterwards.

I can send you the TMM template and planner in electronic form if you want me to.

In the appendix you'll see some TMM outline examples. They are more general than they should be in real life, as I didn't have a specific target audience in mind.

You will do a better job with your efforts, I'm sure.

If you get stuck or if you have a question, feel free to contact me.

The Two-Minute Message

You might want to take advantage of my electronic support service, giving you advice and assistance directly at your time and point of need. Send me your draft letter, message or outline presentation and I'll give you the best feedback I can. I'll have to make a charge, of course, but I'll keep this as low as I can.

When I use the phrase *'have to make a charge'*, I'm not being totally honest. I don't *have to* – I just think I ought to. I'm sure you agree.

I'm happy to give lectures or run seminars and clinics on my TMM process for any number of people. Anything from half an hour to half a day. Once again, get in touch and we can chat about this – probably for more than two minutes. Keep clicking on www.TwoMinuteMessage.com to get the latest information.

Thank you very much for your time. I hope your investment of this precious resource helps you to make better use of it in future.

All good wishes,

William Freeman
Telephone +44 (0)20 8941 9156
williamfreeman@btconnect.com
www.TwoMinuteMessage.com
www.ElevatorPitch.co.uk
www.cambridge-associates.co.uk

14. APPENDICES

The TMM Template

This first part of this appendix contains a blank template and a copy with a brief description of what goes into each of its section.

Use this document to sort out your ideas for a spoken or written TMM, and to put them in sequence. You can enlarge it, or just use the headings in a free-form way, or in some way that suits you. There's no rocket science in this document layout, but most people find it useful.

Email me if you would like a pukka, A4 electronic copy of this template.

Get your basic ideas sorted out first before you worry about the precise words or phrasing that you intend to use.

BUILDING YOUR TWO MINUTE MESSAGE

TMM Topic	
Target Audience	*Intended Outcome*
Audience Context Statement	
Key Theme	
Supporting Themes	
Closing Statement	

BUILDING YOUR TWO MINUTE MESSAGE
EXPLANATION OF TEMPLATE

TMM Topic	
This is the working title of your topic. It is for your eyes only, you'll think of fancier words to use with your audience	
Target Audience	*Intended Outcome*
The specific individual you want to raise the subject with. Named individual if possible	The outcome that you want from your TMM. What do you want your audience to agree to as a result of it?
Audience Context Statement	
Scene setting statements. Significant business issue or implication that you think your audience would (readily) agree to. Nothing about you or your company here. Typically your ACS will come from your knowledge about the client / situation, experiences elsewhere, research or informed opinion, what you have been told, your area of expertise.	
Key Theme	
The main point of your message. The single point that you would want your audience to remember. It will tend to be a clear statement of what you do and the value the recipient gets. This theme should logically follow from the audience context statement. Key themes are rarely unique. Real uniqueness and value tends to show in the supportive detail.	
Supporting Themes	
a) Evidence (e.g. references) to support your key theme and show your capability, credibility and uniqueness (if possible) b) Other significant themes that address the audience context statement and help you achieve your objective	
Closing Statement	
A link back to your objective. A statement of what you would like to happen next	

TMM Examples

The first three examples show the TMM format applied to itself. That sounds somewhat convoluted, so let me explain.

They each take the TMM process as their topic, but look at it from three different angles. You will see how each TMM example differs, according to the intended audience and the desired objective.

The first of these examples is aimed at book publishers. The purpose of this TMM is to interest them (or at least one of them) in the possibility of publishing a book about this topic. My objective is to get a publisher to want to see the idea in more detail. In the terminology of this book, I am buying time to present my case fully. I don't expect my brief letter to get me a publishing contract. Frederick Forsyth might be able to do that, but I cannot.

What I do want, however, is *genuine* interest. This can be difficult to assess, but I know that book publishers are busy people and, in most cases, would not pursue a project unless they thought the idea had merit. You need a bit of trust and faith sometimes (even with book publishers!).

The TMM proforma identifies the key points that I would make (did make, I think). The next step is to take these ideas and draft an appropriate letter, and you'll see my attempt.

There are many ways to skin a cat, of course, so I am not always one hundred percent wedded to exact TMM structure with every letter. But I'm fairly close to it, and any variation is done for a reason.
In this letter I say, up front to these publishers, that I am trying to interest them in a potential book.

They would expect that. They would want that.

BUILDING YOUR TWO MINUTE MESSAGE
BOOK PROPOSAL

TMM Topic	
The Two Minute Message	
Target Audience	*TMM Objective*
Book publishers	To interest them in the potential of a book on this subject, to the extent that they are keen to view a business case and an outline synopsis
Audience Context Statement	
In the competitive business world people constantly need to improve their skills. A new book on a relevant topic has a potential marketplace of many thousands of UK sales people, plus thousands more overseas.	
Key Theme	
The subject of this book (the TMM technique) shows how people can engage the attention of busy clients (in competition with other demands) and earn the extra time they need to present their case. Most sales skills books (and courses) comment on the importance of this activity. This book (unlike any other) focuses on this critical skill.	
Supporting Themes	
The book is designed to be around 100 pages, easy to read and with a style and target price that not only fits the business community, but is sufficiently general to be a good 'impulse buy' for a much wider field. The author's working background and experience give the credibility needed to write such a book. He is also a part-time professional cartoonist and this book would come with accompanying illustrations.	
Closing Statement	
A detailed synopsis is available for consideration and the first draft would be available for consideration within two weeks.	

THE TMM LETTER: BOOK PROPOSAL

Dear Publisher

<u>Proposed Book: The Two Minute Message</u>

I am writing to see if you would be interested in considering publishing this book. It addresses an unexploited niche in the marketplace and is relevant to many thousands of sales people within the UK and abroad.

Sales people are constantly competing for the time and the attention of their clients, and they face fierce competition in doing so. This book describes a technique that will help get the extra time they need to present their case. Unlike any other it focuses on this critical skill.

The book will be around 100 pages, easy to read and with a style and target price that will make it attractive to any businessperson. It will also to be a good 'impulse buy' for a much wider marketplace.

My background and experience gives me the credibility and knowledge to write such a book. I worked many years for IBM as a sales manager and, in my latter years with them, I ran the UK sales training department. In my current role as managing director of Cambridge Associates, I work with other blue-chip organisations helping them to develop their sakes and marketing skills.

If, like me, you are excited by the potential of this book, I would be delighted to send you a synopsis and I could have a sample chapter ready within two weeks. I am keen to move quickly on this project.

Thank you for your time and I look forward to hearing from you. I enclose a stamped addressed envelope for your reply.

Yours sincerely

William Freeman
(keen as mustard and raring to go)

EXAMPLE 2

The second TMM example is also about the two minute message process and it is aimed at people like you, the readers of this book.

It is designed to arouse your interest and curiosity about this topic to the extent that you would want to read the book (or at least flick through it).

I hope you see the importance of the audience context statement. If this doesn't apply to you, or if you think it irrelevant, it is unlikely that you would be attracted to this subject.

If my TMM was successful, you would want to know more about the two minute message process and how you could benefit from it. I hope that it would turn a browser of this book into a buyer of it. So I should put this message where people can see it. Perhaps on the flyleaf.

Even if you have read the book, you might want to know more about the topic or how to develop your skills further - hence my closing statement.

As with the previous example, you will note that the TMM proforma helps to identify the key components of the message. We still need to write the words as they would appear in the letter, book flyleaf or wherever.

If we intend our TMM as part of a face to face or telephone conversation, then we would need to be comfortable about the words and phrasing that we will use, so it becomes part of a natural sounding conversation.

BUILDING YOUR TWO MINUTE MESSAGE
A TMM DESCRIBING THIS BOOK

TMM Topic	
The two minute message concept (the essence of this book)	
Target Audience Busy customer-facing people Potential readers of this book	*Intended Outcome* Arouse their interest in the TMM concept so that they would want to find out more
Audience Context Statement As a business person, you are very busy and so are your clients. You are competing for their time and attention and it is critical to your business success that you can do this	
Key Theme The two minute message process is unique in giving you the ability to crystallise any important 'sales message' into a synopsis that will help you engage the interest of your target audience	
Supporting Themes It is a process that has been tried and proven with a broad cross section of sales people and organisations, each with a variety of sales messages It is easy to learn and will help you to save personal time in constructing your sales propositions, business cases and formal presentations The author of the book has worked with numerous 'blue chip' sales organisations and this book distils his knowledge and experiences into an easy to read format	
Closing Statement The process is described in this book with many illustrations and examples. Even when you have read it you are not alone, you can get further information (and on-line assistance) by visiting www.cambridge-associates.co.uk or by telephoning 020 8941-9156	

EXAMPLE 3: A SET - PIECE MESSAGE

This third example still has the two-minute message technique as its topic. This time I am imagining a situation where someone would ask, "summarise for me how I go about writing a two minute message."

In this example our questioner understands the concept of a TMM but wants an overview on how to write one. In the book we referred to this as a set-piece message.

EXAMPLE 3
A 'SET PIECE' MESSAGE ON HOW TO BUILD A TMM

TMM Topic	
Summary of how to build a two minute message	
Target Audience	*Intended Outcome*
Person who asks the question	Summarise the TMM technique so that the questioner is reminded of the key principles (or told them for the first time)

Audience Context Statement

The underlying principle is based on the fact that you and your clients are busy people. A key part of your job is to compete for, and win, the time and attention of your key customers - internal and external. The TMM process is *the* most effective way to help you do that.

Key Theme

The TMM process enables you to build an effective synopsis of our story, so you can:
a) gain your customers interest and get agreement to further discussion
b) put over a 'set piece' message
c) send a promotional letter
d) use it as a focus for planning a larger event (e.g. a presentation)

Supporting Themes

You start by following the principles of the 'OATS' acronym (define Objective, analyse Audience, identify Themes, create Synopsis)

The four point synopsis consists of Audience Context Statement, followed by your key theme, your supporting themes and closing with a statement that links to your objective

Closing Statement

Of course, nothing will *guarantee* an effective outcome - but following these simple TMM guidelines will help you to construct the most effective possible message with the minimum impact on your time

EXAMPLE 4:

THE VALUE OF USING EXTERNAL CONSULTANTS

As you might imagine, this message is fairly dear to my heart. As an independent consultant, people pay for my time and so I must make sure that they get measurable value in return.

Before all of that can take place, however, I need to sell the value of my services, and I must persuade the client that it is worth considering using external consultants to support the activities of his internal resources (or in some cases, replace those activities).

The old chestnut about a consultant being someone 'who borrows our watch to tell you the time (and then doesn't return it)', implies that consultants don't add value, they just do a job of work that clients could do for themselves. For some of my assignments, I would have to put my hands in the air and plead guilty, but I maintain that clients get value from using temporary resources. More importantly, they would too.

Anyway, this next example shows how a consultant offering IT and business skills could try to sell his potential value to an appropriate customer executive. If you are in this line of business, by all means steal any ideas that you think would help you but as you know by now, you will need to tailor your message to a specific audience.

EXAMPLE 4:
THE VALUE OF USING EXTERNAL CONSULTANTS

TMM Topic	
The value of using external consultants	
Target Audience	*Intended Outcome*
Customer Executive (e.g. IS Director or HR director)	To raise the topic of using external consultancy resources; to get the customer to consider using them on an imminent project

Audience Context Statement
The constantly emerging new technologies demand new ways of working to exploit them. You need to do this to maintain your competitive edge. This requires you to have the 'right' combination of skills at the 'right' time'; skills to plan, design, implement and support your new approach.

Key Theme
Our external consultancy organisation gives you access to skills and resources as and when you need them. We provide resources to complement your in-house skills on short or long term contracts; whatever suits you best.

Supporting Themes
Our partnership network gives us access to a wide variety of resources and skill sets (almost unlimited)
Our work with other clients keeps our technology and industry knowledge up to date; we will understand your problem and know how to resolve it

Closing Statement
With your current projects, you can plan to use your internal resources in the best possible way, in the knowledge that specialist skills can be made available to you, via our consultancy group. We would like to discuss with you how we could add value to your current project.....